QUÉBEC

QUÉBEC

Photography and text by J. A. Kraulis

Whitecap Books
North Vancouver, B.C.

Canadian Cataloguing in Publication Data
Kraulis, J. A., 1949-
   Quebec

   ISBN 0-920620-34-5

   1. Quebec (Province) — Description and travel —
Views. I. Title.
FC2912.K73   917.14'044'0222   C82-091331-6
F1052.8.K73

Copyright © Whitecap Books Ltd.

First edition 1982

Published by
**Whitecap Books Limited,
Ste 1, 431 Mountain Highway,
North Vancouver, B.C.
V7J 2L1.**

ISBN 0-920620-42-6 (French Edition)
ISBN 0-920620-34-5 (English Edition)

Designed by Michael Burch

Printed and bound by D. W. Friesen and Sons Ltd.

Colour separations by Jack Berger Ltd.

Aerial photography on pages 26, 38, 39, 60, 61, 70, 71,
and 79 coproduced with Bo Curtis.

Photo page 78 Andris Rudzitis

Printed in Canada

An Introduction to the Province of Quebec

Quebec is a land of many rivers. More than a thousand strong, they course north, south, east and west in equal abundance, bouncing down the hard granite of the vast Canadian Shield or rushing out of the northern Appalachian Mountains.

A large number remain untouched by settlement or by road; many of these have yet to be explored by even the paddle of a single canoe, having been mapped into existence by aerial survey only in the last few decades. Though their beds are made of some of the oldest stone on earth, almost all of these rivers are wild and young, taking paths determined by the great ice sheet that squashed the land and only entirely melted from it a mere sixty or seventy centuries ago.

Some of Quebec's rivers have been strategically dammed, their restless energy redirected along hundreds of kilometres of high tension aluminum cables to power the diverse wants of an ambitious society. Some serve as cheap conveyor belts for thousands of acres of floating pulpwood shaved here and there from a land bristling with the tight short growth of extensive spruce forests. A few have played the ancient role of rivers in the building of nations by serving as roads for exploration, settlement and trade. On the other hand, many are of no immediate consequence to the majority of Quebecers, relevant perhaps only in the lives of a small number of outdoorsmen seeking good fishing or the ultimate in wilderness whitewater adventure.

One river, the St. Lawrence, is greater than all the rest. Old but mighty, slow but steady, it is the most significant stream in all of North America, both with reference to the past discovery and development of the continent as well as by virtue of its current economic importance.

As befits so stately a stream, the St. Lawrence is never small. Several kilometres wide at its proper source where it leaves Lake Ontario amidst a myriad of islands, it tries on several different sizes: widening at Lac Saint-François where it enters the province, joining with the Ottawa River to embrace the islands at Montreal with a number of lakes and channels, regrouping downstream, then lazily stretching out again at fourteen kilometre wide Lac Saint-Pierre before resetting a more compact course. Just before the river fans out beyond Ile d'Orléans, its silent, awesome current is concentrated between high banks on either side. In the Algonkian language, this is "Kebec", the place "where the river narrows". This is the location of Quebec City.

Today, two giant single span bridges cross the river just upstream of the capital. The newest of the pair, named for Pierre Laporte and sporting massive white concrete towers, is the largest suspension bridge in Canada. Next to it stretches the enormous dark steel truss of the Quebec

Bridge, the longest cantilever span in the world, which was finally completed in 1917 after it had collapsed twice during construction and taken nearly ninety lives.

Side by side, these two engineering monuments seem to physically lash the opposite shores together, as if straining to prevent the widening mouth of the St. Lawrence from splitting the river banks apart completely; for downstream from Quebec, the river spreads ever wider and wider into a great estuary. Too broad to resist the incursion of the sea, its waters become increasingly saline as each shore recedes further and further from the other, dropping beyond the visible horizon.

A glance at a map of North America shows the outline of the St. Lawrence estuary resembling that of a great elongated funnel, with its lip tilted towards Europe and its base directed at the heart of North America. Indeed, the resemblance is not in shape alone. Over the last few centuries, ships carrying explorers, settlers and goods have poured up the St. Lawrence to a degree perhaps unequalled on any other river.

Jacques Cartier became the first recorded explorer to visit the interior of the continent when he discovered and named the St. Lawrence in 1535. On this, the second of his three voyages to North America, he sailed to the Indian village of Stadacona (the present site of Quebec City), and proceeded on as far as Hochelaga, now Montreal. For many of the subsequent explorers the St. Lawrence was a gateway into the continent: Samuel de Champlain, the founder of New France; his two young lieutenants, Étienne Brûlé and Jean Nicolet; Louis Joliet, who established that the Mississippi flowed south; the Sieur de La Salle, who explored the Mississippi to its mouth, and claimed Louisiana for France; the Sieur de la Vérendrye, who broke through the Shield and crossed the Great Lakes watershed to the prairies; not to mention scores of "coureurs des bois" who extended the tendrils of the fur trade network.

The first settlers, as well as waves of later immigrants, came to Canada up the St. Lawrence, along whose banks farmers were clearing the land and tilling the soil more than a century and a half before the first European navigators had even sighted the west coast of British Columbia. Probably most Canadians, and certainly most Quebecers, owe their existence in this country to a voyage up the St. Lawrence, made either personally or by their ancestors.

The flow of commerce through the funnel of the St. Lawrence has gone both ways. From the European prospect, the outline of the estuary might have been more suggestive of a giant cornucopia discharging rich cargoes of beaver pelts, followed by seemingly limitless quantities of timber squared from the large trees which once covered eastern Canada.

It is by virtue of present day commerce that the St. Lawrence deserves to be ranked as one of the great inland waterways of the world. Combined with the Great Lakes, their connecting rivers and the canals and locks of the St. Lawrence Seaway, it allows deep-water ships to reach ports almost 4,000 kilometres from the ocean. It is a rare moment during the shipping season when one can stand on one of the bridges crossing the river at Montreal, Trois Rivières or Quebec City and not see a large freighter with its numerous crane masts, a container ship or one of the long lakers that shuttles grain to downstream ports.

Of the top seven Canadian ports in terms of tonnage handled, only Vancouver is not dependent on the St. Lawrence River.

The St. Lawrence is an international river, afloat with the ships of dozens of nations, and today just as important to Chicago, Detroit and Cleveland as it is to Montreal and Quebec City. But along its shores, most of it is a distinctively French Canadian river.

Travelling down the river one could know, even without knowledge of the landmarks, when one was in Quebec. Shortly after entering the province, leaving behind Ontario on the left and New York on the right bank, one comes to the dam at Beauharnois, where two of the most identifiable symbols of Quebec are prominently on display. On the flat ground just below the dam on the right, landscaped out of grass and concrete, is a representation of the fleur-de-lis flag the size of a football field. Nearly as much a symbol of Quebec, albeit a more prosaic one, is the corporate logo posted on the hydroelectric installations here. A stylized "Q", a simple circle with a lightning bolt, represents Hydro Quebec, the most profitable corporation and individual economic force in the province, responsible for some of the most ambitious and durable engineering works on earth.

The Beauharnois Dam is a monument to the might of the St. Lawrence, for the fall in the river is very slight here. The difference in level, or head, on which water power depends would not warrant a dam on any lesser river, and the Beauharnois Dam, which also serves to deepen the Seaway channel above it, is readily bypassed by two locks on the Beauharnois canal. In spite of this, Beauharnois is the province's second most powerful generating station, its capacity of 1,574,260 kilowatts second only to that of massive LG-2 at James Bay. What the St. Lawrence lacks in height here, it more than makes up for in sheer push; the thirty-six turbines have access to the flow of nearly a cubic kilometre of water every day.

Other signs of Quebec along the river are less direct but more pervasive and perhaps even more durable. The influence of the Roman Catholic religion is always in view. Even the smallest town is dominated by a tall church, its silver-painted single or twin steeples soaring heavenward in sharp contrast to the gently rolling landscape and the wide, flat river. At Montreal, a large cross perches atop Mount Royal, becoming especially conspicuous when outlined against the night sky by the scores of light bulbs around its perimeter. A cross or a statue of Saint Mary invariably occupies every major promontory along the river.

The pervasiveness of religion is everywhere evident in Quebec. Reference to the index of a road map will confirm what the observant reader of town signs would suspect, namely that half of all the communities in the province are named after saints.

Even without its religious symbols, Quebec betrays its identity in little details, such as the ubiquitous sturdy farmhouse so characteristic of rural Quebec. Stout, quadrangular, traditionally built of stone, and with a steeply-pitched gable roof that often ends in a graceful curve at the eaves, many of these unassuming buildings are easily older than any of the cities in Canada west of Winnipeg. Many, on the other hand, are being built and it is not unusual to find their traditional form proudly copied in some suburban home.

At the time of year approaching the summer solstice, another type of structure temporarily becomes common along the banks of the St. Lawrence. Mostly resembling teepees in size and shape, large stacks of firewood, occasionally topped off with an old tire or two, indicate that Quebec's "national holiday", the festival of St. Jean Baptiste, is near. Each year on the night of June 24, the banks of the St. Lawrence and community parks throughout the province are ablaze with hundreds of spectacular bonfires.

Of all the signs of Quebec culture and tradition along the St. Lawrence, perhaps none is as striking as that etched in the soil itself. The seigneurial system of farmland division into long lots makes parts of Quebec distinguishable even from the distant prospect of a satellite.

Along the roads paralleling the river, each farmhouse, accompanied by its barn and workshed, is only a few dozen metres from the next, with a dozen or more seemingly prosperous farms within a single kilometre. Though not large by prairie standards, these farms are not as small as their frontage suggests; they are very narrow, but also very long.

As in so many other aspects of Quebec, the reason for these long farms was the St. Lawrence River itself. When Quebec, then New France, was colonized, the river was its only road. In a feudal system of community, title to tracts of land along the river was granted to seigneurs, who parcelled it out to the farming habitants in such a manner that each would have access to the river. Geometrically, the only possible result was long, narrow lots, which evolved into even thinner strips when a farmer passed his property down to his sons.

Later, when all the riverfront had been exploited, and roads were built, another tier, or "rang", of long lots was carved out of the woods beyond the first. When viewed from above, the resulting pattern gives the St. Lawrence valley the appearance of a giant cloth, elegantly woven in stripes of varying greens and browns.

Most of the farms in Quebec flourish near its southern border. Surrounding Montreal is the widest expanse of the St. Lawrence Lowlands, the fertile plains which settled out of the murky sediments of the Champlain Sea at the end of the Ice Age. The dominance of dairy farming is evident from the profusion of barns and silos. Crops include corn and other grains, vegetables, and in the neighbourhood of the town of Joliette, tobacco. On the gravelly slopes near the Lake of Two Mountains to the west of Montreal and around the individually isolated volcanic domes of the Monteregian Hills to the west, apple orchards are found in profusion.

Downriver, past the last bridges at Quebec, the amount of good farmland diminishes quickly, constrained by the escarpment of the Canadian Shield on the north shore and the Appalachians on the south. Arable land disappears completely in sections along the precipitous shore of the Gaspé Peninsula where the sole road must depend on causeways for passage.

The St. Lawrence estuary is more sea than river. Fringed with slippery mats of seaweed, its deeper waters are a sanctuary for great whales. As agriculture reverts to the barest subsistence farming, fishing boats replace tractors. In opportune places, fish are caught in weirs, netted barricades constructed of a row of large, anchored stakes, sometimes turning back on itself on both sides so as to direct the fish into a circular trap.

As the distance between the opposite shores of the St. Lawrence increases, so do the differences between them. The south shore is dotted with small fishing villages, culminating in the picturesque coastline of the Gaspé Peninsula, while the north shore is wilder and larger, with the timber and mineral resources of the Canadian Shield in its backyard.

At Baie-Comeau, on the north shore, aluminum and pulp and paper mills take advantage of the abundant hydroelectric power from the nearby Manicouagan and Outardes Rivers. At Sept-Iles, ships take on dense cargoes of iron ore pellets with such frequency that in some years this remote town has qualified as Canada's number one international seaport in the strictly statistical category of most tonnage. The harbour at nearby Port-Cartier handles comparable quantities of iron ore, and its big storage elevators, like those at Baie-Comeau, serve to transfer grain from the lakers to the holds of sea-going vessels.

Along the north shore beyond Sept-Iles, a scattering of isolated settlements continues eastward and northward, serviced only by air or sea. Along this coast, beyond Anticosti Island, the St. Lawrence River seems far away. The land is as rough and as lonely as the sea waters of the wide Gulf of St. Lawrence.

At Blanc-Sablon, the easternmost part of Quebec, the Strait of Belle Isle separates the island of Newfoundland from Quebec and the rest of Canada. It is through this passageway that ships taking the shortest route from Europe first arrived in North America. Blocked by ice from November to June, menaced by nearby icebergs in summer, and flanked by rocky, windswept terrain, desolate but for its stunted trees, the strait hardly presents a hospitable welcome. Through it sailed Jacques Cartier on his first voyage, anchoring off Blanc-Sablon several days before his landing at Gaspé. His first impressions of Quebec were not particularly favourable; it was, he observed in an oft-quoted remark, "the land God gave to Cain."

While the north shore gradually tapers off into wilderness, the south shore of the St. Lawrence estuary ends with sudden, heart-stopping abruptness. The Gaspé Peninsula terminates in a smaller peninsula, which in turn ends in a long, narrow finger of land, at the very tip of which Cap Gaspé drops sheer and overhanging, 100 metres straight into the sea. Nearby Cap Bon Ami, 200 metres high, is even more impressive. The place would perhaps be more popularly known were it not for Quebec's most famous landmark, twenty-five kilometres away.

Strong and monolithic in form, of simply chiseled texture, dramatic and sure in gesture, Percé Rock suggests the work of some giant sculptor: a great stylized ship of rusty gold, a symbolic monument placed to mark the gateway to a continent. Like most monuments, this one is associated with events of destiny. Not far away, Jacques Cartier made his famous landing at Gaspé, meeting with a group of Iroquois and erecting a cross in honour of his king, an event that marks the textbook beginning of New France in 1534. Several generations later, Samuel de Champlain, the true father of New France, named the rock as he sailed past it on his way to establishing the habitation that would become Quebec City. The first naval battle in North America took place near the rock when British ships ambushed arriving French settlers.

However, it is for its natural history rather than the human history of its environs that Percé Rock is especially noteworthy. Built of some 400 million fossils, the 500 metre long rock serves as home for hundreds of sea birds which nest on its flat top, although its ample gull and cormorant population seems sparse in comparison to the fifty thousand gannets that comprise one of the world's largest such colonies on close-by Bonaventure Island.

The best known feature of the rock is perhaps the twenty metre high archway that passes right through it at water level. The rock derives its name from such piercings. A more impressive opening existed as recently as 1854 when the large archway spanning the rock and the pillar that now stands at its seaward end collapsed. Early explorers reported as many as four piercings. Constantly changing, itself a remnant of a once greater shoreline, Percé Rock provides stark evidence of the power of the alliance of time and the sea.

No doubt the greatest influence of the St. Lawrence on Quebec's destiny has been in its role in the founding of two of North America's most distinctive cities, Quebec City and Montreal. The site of the former, where the funnel of the St. Lawrence estuary narrows down to river size, is of singular historical importance. Here Champlain, the greatest of the early explorers and colonists, established what would become the oldest permanent European settlement on the continent. In 1608, he built his "Abitation" at the base of the steep escarpment whose crest commands a sweeping, majestic view of the river and which, not incidentally, was the first location coming upstream where cannon fire could effectively sweep the full width of the water route. While the stone at Percé elegantly marks the gateway to North America, Quebec City was destined to guard the actual door.

Its strategic role was underscored several times when it hosted pivotal battles in the struggle for administrative control of the continent. Today, several dozen plaques and monuments in National Battlefields Park on the Plains of Abraham commemorate past conflicts, the first and most famous of which occurred in 1759. While the British won the battle against the defending French, the commanders of both forces, General Wolfe and General Montcalm, died in the fight, poignantly emphasizing the fact that though there were differences between the French and English — their destinies on this great continent were inevitably linked.

Quebec City is at the crossroads between the sea and the land. Its role as one of the major ports of entry for immigration has somewhat diminished with modern air travel, but its maritime connection is as present as ever. Five-metre tides gently rock a busy waterfront. Most conspicuous among the docked ships are those from the red and white fleet of the Canadian Coast Guard. This is the home port for some of Canada's powerful icebreakers, including those which crash up and down the St. Lawrence to force open the passage to Montreal for most of the winter. Across the river at Lauzon, welders assemble ships at the Davy Shipyards, the largest in Canada.

In the summertime, tourists invade the town in numbers that would have astonished the old defenders of this, the only walled city in North America. The well-preserved courtyards, colourful roofs and abundant steeples, culminating in the peaks and turrets of the palatial Chateau Frontenac: all give Quebec City a charm unequalled in North America.

Impressive statues are numerous, honouring famous men and women, most of them former citizens of this city. One monument commemorates Louis Hébert, the first European farmer in North America. Another represents Monseigneur de Laval, Canada's first bishop, a most eminent man of many achievements including the founding of the Quebec Seminary from which grew Laval University. Yet another statue reproduces the likeness of George Étienne Cartier, eloquent spokesman of French rights and one of the Fathers of Confederation. Of course, the most ambitious of all honours Champlain. High above the St. Lawrence and Place Royale, the multi-figure monument at the end of Dufferin Terrace shows the great man in mid-stride, hat in hand as if just disembarking in the new land.

While Quebec City has charm and character, built on the strength of its culture and history, Montreal has the excitement of a large, cosmopolitan city. With an authentic old town, and more French speaking people than any other city in the world except Paris, it has its own ancestral claim to the proud heritage and traditions of the province.

Two of the great international celebrations which focus attention on a single place are the World's Fair and the Olympics. Montreal is the only city of this century to have hosted both. Montreal is also the home of the National Theatre School, and boasts four universities: McGill, the University of Montreal, Concordia, and a branch of the University of Quebec. Other northern cities have followed its innovative plan of an underground indoor city-within-a-city; the weatherproof shop-and-restaurant lined corridors of Place Ville Marie and subsequent similar developments.

The island city with the mountain in its midst owes its stature and its existence to the St. Lawrence. The river has only a few dozen metres to descend from Montreal to tidewater, which it reaches halfway to Quebec City at Trois-Rivières. Deep-drafting ocean ships have always been able to sail straight to Montreal, where the obstruction presented by the Lachine Rapids helped turn it into a major terminus.

At the same time, its position at the mouth of the Ottawa River ensured its pre-eminence soon after de Maisonneuve founded it in 1642 as the settlement of Ville-Marie-de-Mont-Royal. The Ottawa River was the main avenue for the lucrative fur trade which dominated the economy of New France right up to the time when it was ceded to British administration.

Far removed from the sea, with not a trace of salt in the air, Montreal nonetheless remains one of the world's major port cities. Perhaps only the winter which freezes its harbour has restrained it from burgeoning on the scale of New York.

With a metropolitan population of two and a half million, more than a third the total of all of Quebec, Montreal ranks as Canada's most populous city. If one includes the inhabitants of the surrounding plain within an hour's drive of the city, then the Montreal region accounts for well over half of the total population of the province.

Such a concentration of numbers, not to mention cultures, makes it impossible to easily describe the region. As a manufacturing centre, its goods, from textiles and packaged foods to automobiles and aircraft, are too diverse to summarize. So are its entertainments: its clubs, theatres, festivals, and the ethnic diversity of its outstanding restaurants.

Montreal is also noteworthy as a sports capital, a tradition anchored by its claim to the most successful hockey team in the history of the sport, the Canadiens. Although not as established as the Canadiens, the Montreal Expos of the National Baseball League draw large crowds at the Olympic Stadium. With the new Concordes of the Canadian Football League, and the Manic of the North American Soccer League, the city is one of the few in North America to boast four professional sports teams.

An Olympic rowing basin and a Grand Prix racetrack built on the artificial island of Ile-Notre-Dame and an architecturally amazing velodrome are among the exotic world-class facilities left as the legacy of the World's Fair and the Olympics. The race track, named for the late Gilles Villeneuve, winds through Man and His World, an exhibition and entertainment park set amidst the well-preserved pavilions of Expo 67. Each year it hosts the glamour and the thunder of the Grand Prix, the ultimate in auto racing.

So much of Quebec is the St. Lawrence, and yet another glance at the map shows that Quebec is so much more than the St. Lawrence. The river valley in which dwell most of the province's people occupies but a small percentage of the area of this far-reaching land.

Chief among Quebec's other regions are those served by the tributaries of the St. Lawrence. The largest of these is the Ottawa River. Shared by Ontario and Quebec, it is, like the St. Lawrence, a reminder both symbolic and real of the close links between the two provinces.

Back in the days when rivers functioned as roads rather than as barriers to them, it was Champlain and his associates who travelled up the Ottawa, portaging across to the Great Lakes and becoming the first Europeans to establish links with the region that would, centuries later, become Ontario's heartland. Today, some communities on the Ontario side of the river are predominantly French speaking, while areas on the Quebec side have British roots. Most of the Ottawa valley has been surveyed according to a grid, on the English township system. A small enclave of long narrow farms established under the French seigneurial system gives the area around the Petite Nation River a character different from the rest of the Ottawa valley. Nearby at Montebello is a famous hotel, the impressive Chateau Montebello, one of the largest log buildings in the world.

Like most of Quebec's utilized rivers, the Ottawa and tributaries such as the Gatineau, the Lièvre and the Rouge are afloat with pulpwood, and are dammed here and there for hydroelectric power. Away from the pulp mills, the pastoral hill country north of the Ottawa River is full of picturesque little farms, small villages with modest white churches, the occasional covered bridge and abundant secluded woodlands, such as those preserved in Gatineau Park.

The Richelieu River, which joins the St. Lawrence at Sorel, is like a miniature copy of its master stream. Its source is a large lake, Lake Champlain. It served as a road for rural settlement, and the seigneurial system of long lots is particularly well defined along its shores. Moreover, it was a strategically important river, guarded in places such as Fort Lennox and Fort Chambly, both restored as national historic sites. A short river, no part of it being much more than half an hour's drive from Montreal, it belongs entirely to the St. Lawrence Lowlands region.

More independent, yet in many ways another analogy of the St. Lawrence, is the Saguenay River. Like the St. Lawrence, it flows at sea level for much of its length and feels the pulse of the tide far upstream. Ore ships cruise its channel, supplying raw materials to industry built on an immense scale. At the head of navigation, the area around Chicoutimi is to aluminum what Hamilton, Ontario is to steel. The plant at Arvida was for many years the largest producer of aluminum in the world, while another plant operates at the nearby port of La Baie, and a third at Alma. While ships can't reach it, Lac St. Jean is evocative of Lake Ontario, save for its cooler, cleaner air. Here, the black and white of Holstein herds complements a landscape of bright green fields and contrasting dairy farm buildings often trimmed or roofed in red.

Quebec City's Cap aux Diamants overlooking the St. Lawrence has been called the Gibraltar of North America. The Saguenay, too, has its Gibraltar, a much more impressive one that rivals the real thing: Cap Trinité drops four hundred metres of sheer granite into the deep river. A painstakingly constructed hiking trail provides access over and part way down the cape to a viewpoint alongside a nine metre high statue of the Virgin. From this spectacular prospect, however, all temptation to compare the Saguenay with the St. Lawrence dissipates. One is confronted with a river extraordinarily rugged along both shores, a river without a valley; in effect, a wide fjord carved through the Shield and lined with innumerable cliffs of which Cap Trinité is merely one, albeit the highest. One can see twenty kilometres up and down the river, and not a hint of human settlement is in view. While two roads parallel the river, they travel easier terrain far inland. Where the St. Lawrence is a river of civilization, the Saguenay is a river of wilderness.

Historically different from most of the rest of Quebec is its southeastern corner, the Eastern Townships, bordering Vermont, New Hampshire and Maine. Settled by United Empire

Loyalists who fled the American Revolution, its land was surveyed according to the rectangular English township system rather than in the seigneurial manner of long lots in most of the rest of the province's agricultural areas.

Today a cultural mosaic with some forty different ethnic groups, but predominantly French, the Eastern Townships are noted for their artistic vigour. Art centres, music camps, theatres and numerous festivals thrive amidst the rolling countryside, its contours further softened by the green growth and muting haze of summer. Two of Quebec's seven universities, the only ones outside of Quebec City and Montreal, are located here: the University of Sherbrooke and Bishop's University in Lennoxville, which is modelled after England's Oxford.

In direct contrast to the idyllic setting of most of the Townships is the massive monolithic industry at Thetford Mines and Asbestos, where open pits testify to the abundance of asbestos ore below ground. The operation at Asbestos is especially huge; the vast hole of the Jeffrey Mine is the largest open pit asbestos mine in the world. Its dimensions are so great that one is tempted to believe it has served as a giant mold from which the round hills of the nearby Appalachians have been cast.

Like the Loyalists, the Appalachian Mountains are immigrants from the United States. After providing the Eastern Townships with their scenery and some of the finest ski hills in eastern Canada, the mountains saunter northeast, paralleling the St. Lawrence until they come stiffly to attention in the Chic-Choc Range of the Gaspé Peninsula. Here are Quebec's highest easily accessible mountains, with bald tops and steep gullies that remain snow-filled into July. The tallest, predictably named Mont Jacques Cartier, is 1,270 metres above sea level.

From the Chic-Chocs to its dramatic coastline, the Gaspé is the most naturally varied region in Quebec. Nowhere else can one clear one's lungs in the pure alpine air above timberline, intoxicate oneself on the heavy perfume of spruce woods, and breathe salty wind to the rhythm of the sea, all during the course of a single day.

Two hundred and fifty kilometres to the east of the Gaspé Peninsula, out in the middle of the Gulf of St. Lawrence, lie the Magdalen Islands, the smallest, most isolated and perhaps the most different of Quebec's regions. Further removed from other parts of Quebec than they are from Nova Scotia and Prince Edward Island, the Magdalens resemble the latter with its middle removed. They do not have P.E.I.'s peaceful fields, thick with potatoes and grain. On limited land, hay for a scattering of livestock is the only obvious crop, stored here and there in compact cubical piles topped with large, pyramid-shaped plywood hats to keep them dry. For the fishermen who live here, the sea is always close by. The ever present wind races unrestrained across the Gulf and over the islands. It almost seems to have forced prone much of the land, where long flat sand spits interconnect the bare hills of six of the eight main islands.

What the Magdalens lack in interior acreage, however, they more that make up for in perimeter. Their fine sandy beaches are much longer than those for which P.E.I. is famous; their headlands of soft, deep-red sandstone which frame the beaches are higher and more dramatically eroded.

Weighing in with by far the greatest portion of the land area of Quebec is the Canadian Shield, as rough and unyielding as the St. Lawrence is smooth and accessible. On a clear day, the edge of the Shield is always visible from the St. Lawrence. Viewing its low, forested hills is somewhat like looking end-on at the edge of sheet of paper: what one sees totally belies the immense area that lies beyond. If all the regions of Quebec outside the Shield were to be erased from a map of the province, it might take a second look to notice the change. Seven-eighths of the original area would remain — almost everything north and west of the St. Lawrence — as would most of Quebec's distinctive scooped and pointed outline.

Few Quebecers ever get a taste of the true proportions of the land within this outline. Most have only nibbled at the edges, in recreation meccas like the Laurentians north of Montreal. Only forty minutes from the metropolis and full of cottage-lined lakes, summer camps, luxurious lodges, quaint villages, small farms, woodlots for tapping maple syrup, scores of ski hills and one ski mountain (Mont Tremblant), it seems inevitable that the Laurentians should be crowded. By some magic of place, they are not; real estate is still reasonably priced, and one can take long cross-country ski tours or forest walks in surprising solitude.

Wilder and more rugged parklands are found to the north of Quebec City. Along the Jacques Cartier or Malbaie Rivers, flanked with dense forests growing on steep slopes arrayed with cliffs and waterfalls, it is possible to believe that one has been transported to the deep valleys of British Columbia's coast.

The parks of the Shield give but a hint of that portion which lies beyond: the dryland equivalent of the ocean. To drive one of the few roads into the area is like setting out to sea in a small boat; a breakdown would be extraordinarily inconvenient, and to stray even a few dozen metres from one's vehicle is to enter a primeval world where, to lose one's way would be disastrous.

It is a land of nothing but stone, wood and water, yet paradoxically a land of great riches. The stone of the Shield is literally a gold mine in places like Val d'Or and Chibougamou, but also is abundantly loaded with copper, zinc and silver in these and other mining centres like Rouyn-Noranda and Matagami. A few hundred kilometres north of Sept-Iles, a long depression in the Shield called the Labrador Trough contains one of the world's largest deposits of iron ore, mined at Gagnon, Schefferville, Fermont and, in Labrador, Wabush and Labrador City.

The wood of the Shield is equally precious, supplying what in Quebec and in Canada as a whole is one of the largest industries: pulp and paper. The black spruce trees which blanket the southern half of the Shield are small but old; their tightly grown fibre makes for a particularly good grade of pulpwood. Huge booms containing tens of thousands of short logs are towed by tugboat across the slack water of the many reservoirs. They present elegant parachute-like outlines when seen from the prospect of the bush plane or the helicopter, the only practical means of access to most of the Shield.

It is water, the most abundant resource, that has prompted man's most dramatic impact on the Shield. The violent rapids and cascades of rivers are Quebec's "white oil". An eternal source of power, the rivers have been harnessed by structures nearly as permanent. The dams on the Mauricie, Bermisis, Outardes, Manicouagan, La Grande, Eastmain and other rivers are Quebec's Pyramids. Massive, pure of form, several are the largest of their kind. Manic 5, the Daniel Johnson Dam, is the largest multiple-arch dam on earth and arguably the most beautiful. Manic 2, downriver, is the world's largest hollow-joint gravity feed dam. Quebec's hydro reservoirs are also among the world's largest, its transmission lines among the longest.

An enormous manmade cave, the world's largest underground generating station, has been carved out of the rock at LG-2, one of the installations at James Bay. Called "the project of the century", the 5,328 megawatt capacity of the completed half of the James Bay Complex was gained by putting 14,000 men to work diverting some of the north's largest rivers.

The James Bay Complex, like the iron mines, reaches into what is known as New Quebec, a region beyond the dense forests which seem to run northward forever, a region that occupies more than half of all the area of Quebec. Here the spruce trees grow far apart, interspersed with thick, crunchy matts of bleached green caribou moss. String bog, thick braids of turf half floating in tea-coloured water, restricts travel across this open boreal woodland. Further north, the trees become progressively sparser and smaller, until they are little more than scattered clumps of bushes. Taiga turns to tundra as finally the trees disappear altogether. From south of Ungava Bay to Quebec's northern tip at Ivujivik is barren land, nearly as extensive in area as all of Quebec's settled regions combined, and larger than that of the Yukon.

So remote is northern Quebec that the most northerly road, that to the James Bay Complex, reaches a point less than half the latitudinal distance from Quebec's southern border to its northernmost point, further north than the southern tip of Baffin Island. It is a land large enough to hide wonders most people have never heard of: the New Quebec Crater, a great circular cauldron of water created by the impact of an immense meteor; Leaf Basin, where the tides are said to be higher than those in the Bay of Fundy; the barren and sheer Torngat Mountains, the highest in the province. It is a land where polar bears patrol the fringes, where a quarter of a million caribou far outnumber the people, and where in June and July, midnight is merely a deep dusk.

It is called New Quebec because only recently has it become a part of the Quebecer's consciousness; only since 1912 has it been governed from Quebec City. But in a real and true sense, this is oldest Quebec. If the Norse ever saw Quebec, most likely it would have been its northern shore. Since a time long before the Vikings, however, this has been the home of Quebec's original peoples. Today, eight thousand Cree hunt, fish and trap in the interior. Five thousand Inuit are based in scattered settlements along the Arctic coast, representatives of a community that has endured far longer than any European empire.

For all its size and variety, Quebec remains distinctive not so much as a place on the map, but as a state of mind, a blend of traditions as strong as its St. Lawrence and of ambitions as expansive as its north.

It is inextricably a part of North America by virtue of both its physical and economic geography, and indisputably separate from most of the continent by virtue of its language: most Quebecers are not fluent in English while only a small fraction of those outside of Quebec understand French. But while language is all important in the affairs of men — it is the vital breath of community, the taproot of heritage, the tool of power and politics — it serves only as a reference point, and not as the explanation of the state of mind that is Quebec.

It is impossible to generalize about a people without stumbling into pitfalls: oversimplication, contradiction, omission. But French Quebecers share an outlook, a common character that is different from that of the English in Canada. It originates in a strong and deep sense of community, primarily evidenced in the outline of the land. Under the seigneurial system it is possible for today's rural residents, as it was for the first colonists, to visit several neighbours within very near walking distance. The British habit of surveying out square proportioned lots admitted no such possibility.

Most significant, however, is the French Quebecers' consciousness of their roots in the land, roots that reach deeper than those of any other ethnic group in Canada with the exception of the Indians and the Inuit. The last significant immigration of people from France to what is now Quebec took place from 1660 to 1670 under the authority of the intendant Jean Talon. Thus, the ancestors of virtually every French Canadian made the St. Lawrence valley their home more than three hundred years ago. In Canada, Quebec has seniority; even ordinary Hull is an older city than the ostentatious national capital that looks down on it from across the Ottawa River.

The sense of community in Quebec is consistent with the nationalist aspirations of a significant portion of its population, but its meaning is much deeper than the reach of any political movement. Adhering to one's traditions and to one's land is more enduring and far more valuable than any system of government, which is subject to all human whims, weaknesses and prejudices. Many Quebecers proudly fly the fleur-de-lys alongside the Canadian flag without any sense of contradiction, but one of the realities which Canadian federalists must accept is the fact that for most Quebecers, it is Quebec that dwells deepest and strongest in their hearts.

In addition to sharing a sense of community, Quebecers on the whole express themselves in a manner that suggests a lack of self-consciousness and a tolerance of others. It is an engaging quality, famous in the infectious laughter of comedian Yvon Deschamps, manifested silently here and there in a love for extravagant decoration. It is not uncommon to find a home in Quebec embellished in wild hues: a rural dwelling surrounded with dozens of wagon wheels and all aglow in bright yellows and reds; an urban row house with roof, balcony and stairs in a colour scheme that appears to have been inspired by the inside of a kaleidoscope.

In Montreal, it has inspired more of the same on a larger scale. Bright, fantastic murals obscure the blank exterior sides of apartments and warehouses in dozens of locations throughout the city. Dreary façades are turned to advantage in a spirit that values liveliness over order, involvement over propriety.

It is hard, at first, to relate this ingenuous nature of French Quebecers and their inward focusing sense of community to their collective prowess as monument builders, a prowess identified more with stern, humourless empires. Pride in the past, however, begets pride in the future, and in the final analysis, Quebec's great dams, bridges and stadia are entirely in character with the people who moved the first stones, who started the first small farms on the shores of a great river.

Respect for the future of Quebec's most powerful tradition has built great churches of a scale and durability that rival the cathedrals of Europe: the shrines at Sainte-Anne-de-Beaupré, Cap-de-la-Madeleine and St. Joseph's Oratory each attract millions of pilgrims every year, and the dome of St. Joseph's is surpassed in size only by St. Peter's in Rome.

As rich in contrasts as the contradiction of its seasons, as multifaceted and compelling as the flow of its rivers, Quebec is not always a comfortable land, and not a land easy to comprehend. But for those who live in it and for those who don't, but who have come to know and to love it, it is a land one could not do without.

The National Assembly Building, Quebec City.

Above: The rugged coast of the Gulf of St. Lawrence at Pointe-St-Pierre near Gaspé.

Opposite: Previously part of the estate of the late prime minister Mackenzie King, the ruins at Kingsmere are now part of Gatineau Park.

Following pages: The Montreal skyline from the heights of Mount Royal.

Opposite and above: The beauty of a fresh spring season in rural Quebec.

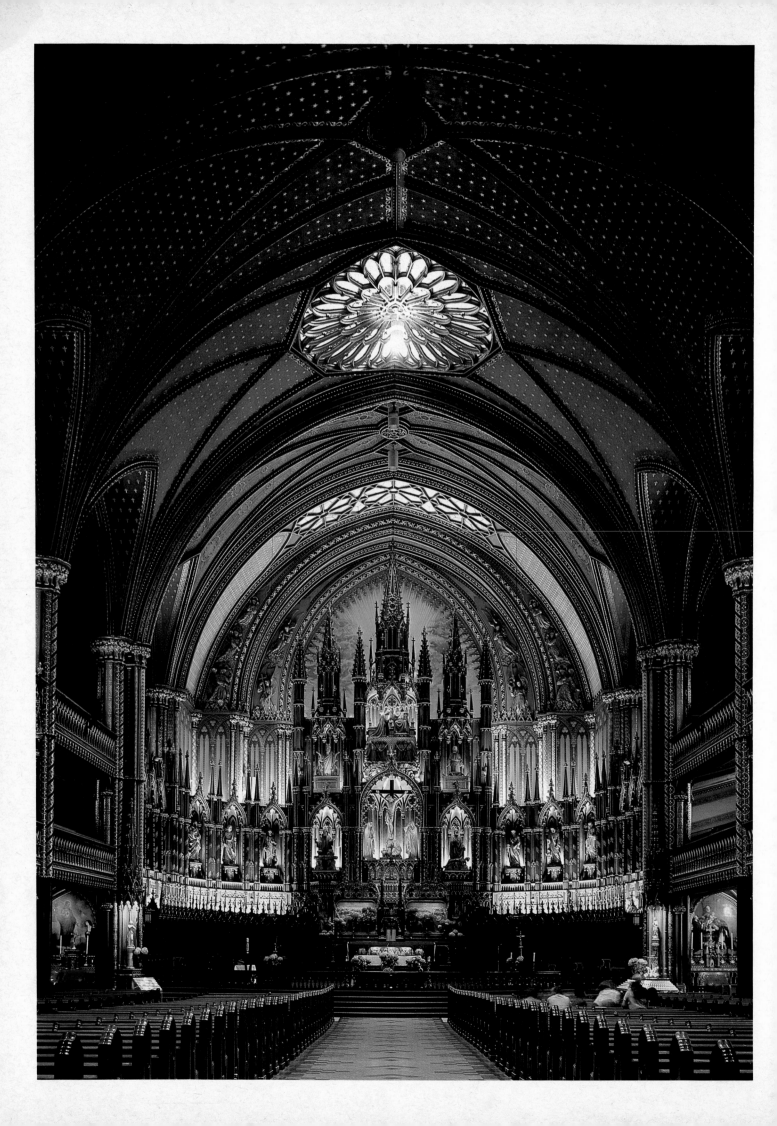

Above: Completed in 1967 St. Joseph's Oratory is Canada's largest church. The octagonal dome is second only in size to that of St. Peter's in Rome.

Opposite: The interior of Notre-Dame Church in Montreal. Completed in 1829, the church is the centre piece of Old Montreal.

Above: The St. Lawrence near Grosses-Roches.

Opposite: Aerial view of the Laurentians.

Opposite and above: The massive bulk of Percé Rock. The French explorer Jacques Cartier is said to have landed near here in 1534.

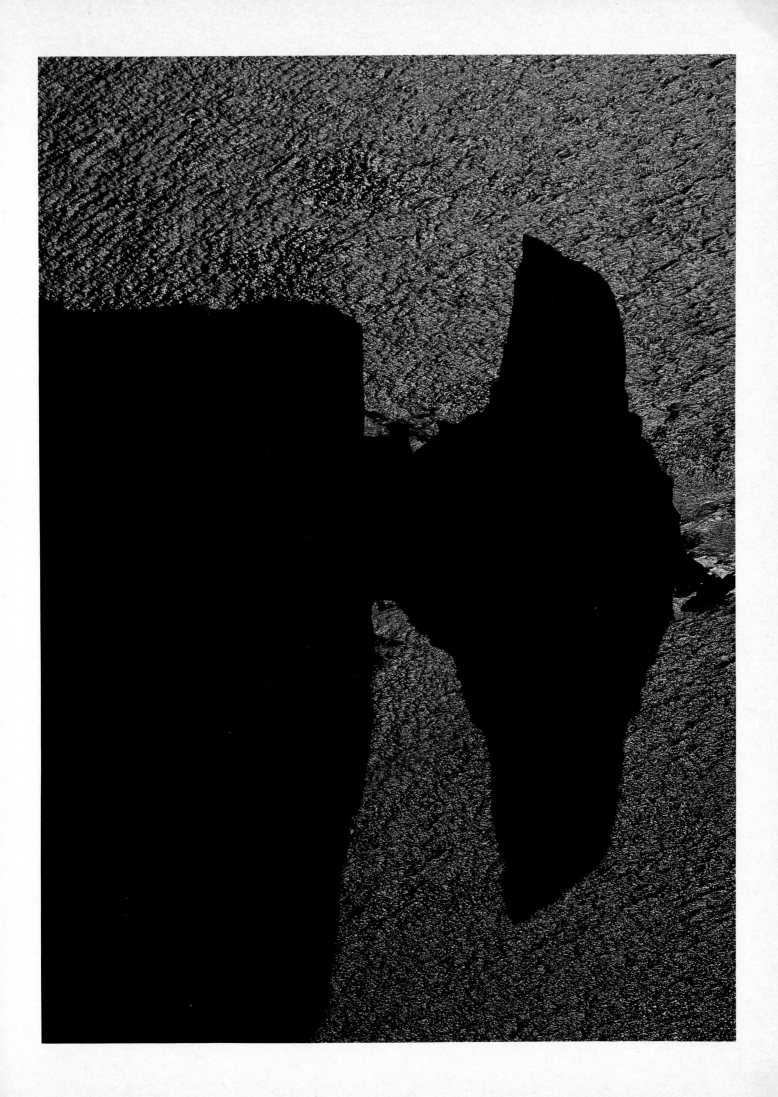

The Olympic Stadium and the surrounding sports complex was built to hold the 1976 Olympic Games. Today the stadium is home for Montreal's professional sports teams and is used for many other special events.

L'Anse-au-Beaufils (above) and Ste.-Thérèse-de-Gaspé (opposite) are two of the numerous fishing villages along the south shore of the Gaspé Peninsula.

Preceding pages: Boats on the Magdalen Islands. The archipeligo consists of a dozen islands in the Gulf of St. Lawrence northeast of Prince Edward Island.

Scenes from the backstreets of Montreal off Prince Albert Street.

Decorated homes at Bic (above) and Ste.-Félicité (below) along
the south shore of the St. Lawrence.

Above: The Turcot Interchange, Montreal.

Opposite: In a feudal system title to tracts of land along the St. Lawrence was granted to seigneurs, who then parcelled out sections to farmers, such that each lot had river frontage. The lots were then divided by other generations resulting in a patchwork of narrow fields seen in this aerial photograph.

Above: The Rue St. Louis is the main thoroughfare of the old part of Quebec City. With its rooming houses and excellent restaurants it is popular with both residents and visitors alike.

Opposite: Farm buildings near Notre-Dame de la Salette.

Cliffs above La Malbaie River.

Rock climbing near Val David.

Above: Hydro Quebec power line at dusk.

Opposite: Aluminum plant at Shawinigan.

Opposite: Place Royale and the Chateau Frontenac. The Chateau Frontenac was built in 1895, and some of the houses in Place Royale date back to the 17th century.

Above: Scenes from old Quebec City.

Following pages: The Quebec City skyline and the St. Lawrence River.

Above: The ghost-town at Val-Jalbert Park was acquired by the provincial government in 1960. Many of the buildings once housed workers from the nearby pulp mill which was forced to close down in 1927.

Opposite: Stream bed near Mont Joli.

Participant in the Caribbean Festival, Montreal.

Street performer at Man and His World, Montreal.

Below: Horses near Harrington in the Laurentians.

Above: Cornfield near Weedon in the Eastern Townships.

Opposite: A small river rushes towards the mighty St. Lawrence at St. Fidèle.

Above: Bonhomme Carnaval in the annual parade in Quebec City. For ten days every February the city discards the drabness of winter and erupts into celebration with dances, winter sports, parades, and many other events.

Opposite: Fireworks in Montreal herald the arrival of evening on St. Jean Baptiste Day, Quebec's public holiday.

These churches are typical examples of the numerous styles found throughout Quebec. The church opposite can be seen on the Ile d'Orleans and the one pictured above is in the Rouge River Valley.

The Sainte Marguerite River north of Sept-Îles.

Open boreal woodland near the Labrador border.

Lighthouse at La Martre, Gulf of St. Lawrence.

Bunchberries, Forillon National Park.

Following pages: Fall colours near Morin Heights.

Above: The village of Rivière-Trois-Pistoles.

Opposite: 19th century mansion in Rivière-du-Loup.

Above: Mont Saint-Bruno, one of the eight peaks of the Monteregian Hills.

Opposite: Ouiatchouane Falls near Lac Saint-Jean.

Above: A laker passes beneath the Laviolette Bridge at Trois-Rivieres on its journey down the St. Lawrence.

Opposite: Pulpwood and hydro-electric power, two of the great resources of the Canadian Shield. A flume permits the passage of logs over the Manic 2 Dam north of Baie-Comeau.

Above: A small dairy farm at Rivington.

Opposite: Autumn in the Laurentians: a mosaic of birch, aspen, spruce and maple near St.-Sauveur-des-Morts.

Above: Salle Wilfrid-Pelletier, home of the Montreal Symphony Orchestra, is the largest of three theatre buildings at Place des Arts.

Opposite: An information kiosk adds colour to Dominion Square in Montreal. Aluminum-clad Place Ville Marie and the city's copper-capped cathedral, Mary Queen of the World, dominate the background.

Winter sports in Quebec are not for the faint of heart. (Above) A frosty faced cross-country ski racer. (Opposite) Freestyle competition at Belle Neige in the Laurentians.

Above: Ice floes in Ungava Bay.

Opposite: Tasisuak Lake in the far north of the province connects
with Nairn Bay.

Opposite: Place Royale and the Petit Champlain at night from Dufferin Terrace in Quebec City.

Above: A small waterfall above the Perron Boulevard along Quebec's east coast.

Above: The Canadian Ski Marathon near Montebello. The two day event, which covers 160 kilometres from Lachute to Hull, is the longest of its kind.

Opposite: Sculpted by cold winter winds, snowdrifts and sastrugi blanket the farm fields on Ile d'Orleans.

Above and Opposite: An early snowfall in November sets the stage for the colour and ceremony of a Grey Cup Parade in Montreal.

Sunset over the St. Lawrence River at Montreal silhouettes the Jacques Cartier Bridge (above) and an old church in Verdun (opposite).

Red sandstone rock off the Magdalen Islands.